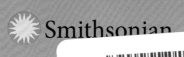

Life on a Farm

Courtney Acampora

Contents

Morning on the Farm

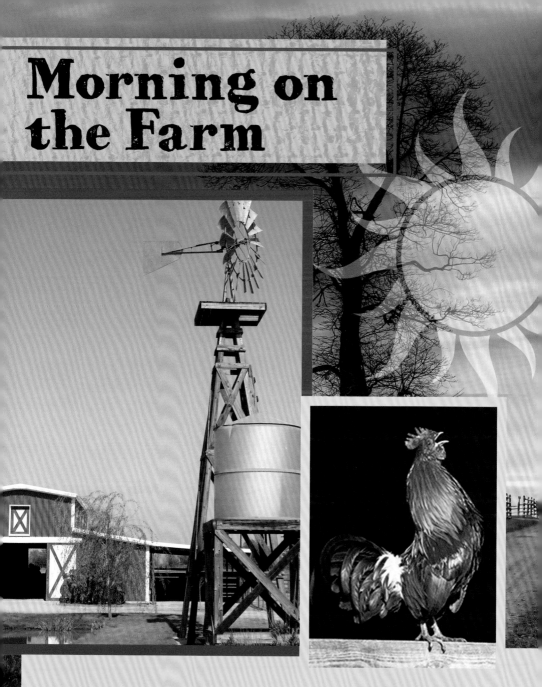

The day begins early on the farm.

The rooster crows "cock-a-doodle-doo!"

Working on the Farm

A farmer works on the farm.

The farmer takes care of the animals and **crops**.

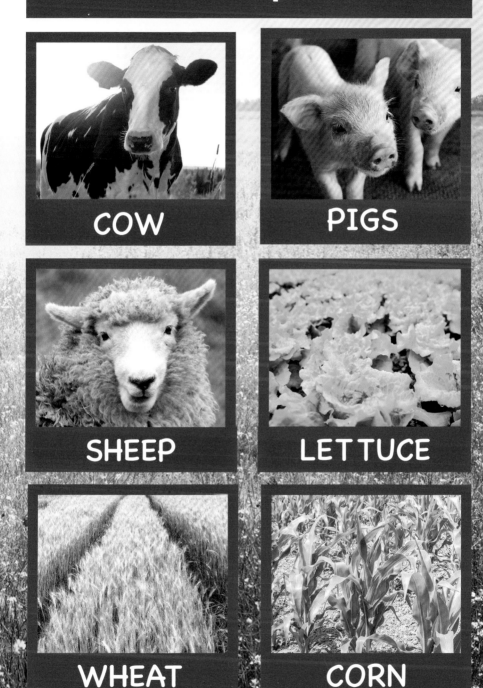

COW

PIGS

SHEEP

LETTUCE

WHEAT

CORN

Growing Crops

Crops grow on the farm.

Tractors are used to **harvest** the crops.

Tractors gather hay for the animals to eat.

Tractors drop seeds into the soil.

The seeds grow into plants!

Big Red Barn

The farm has a big red barn.

Animals sleep in the barn.

Horses

The horses say "neigh!"

They eat hay.

Pigs

Pigs live in a pigpen.

They roll in mud to cool off.

Pigs squeak and squeal!

Chickens

Female chickens are called hens.

Hens lay eggs.

Chickens peck at seeds on the ground.

Cows

Cows eat grass.

Cows say "moo!"

Cows give us milk.

Rabbits

Hop, hop!

Rabbits nibble on grass and carrots.

Ducks

Ducklings swim in a pond.

Ducklings follow their mother.

Goats

Goats have hooves.

Young goats are called kids.

Some goats have horns.

Sheep

Sheep graze in the grass.

Sheep grow thick hair called **wool**.

Wool is used to make clothes.

Sheepdogs

Sheepdogs help **herd** the sheep.

The dog barks "woof, woof!"

Life on a Farm

At night, the animals go to the barn.

Tomorrow will be another busy day!

Life on a Farm
Quiz

1. What do pigs do to cool off?
   - a) Roll in the mud
   - b) Swim in the pond
   - c) Sleep in the barn

2. Where does milk come from?
   - a) Chickens
   - b) Ducks
   - c) Cows

3. What are young goats called?
   a) Hens
   b) Kids
   c) Lambs

4. What animals grow wool?
   a) Sheep
   b) Cows
   c) Goats

Answers: 1) a 2) c 3) b 4) a

GLOSSARY

Crops: plants grown on a farm

Harvest: to gather crops

Herd: to move a group of animals

Wool: sheep hair

Farmer

Goats

Crops

Tractor

Sheep

Ducks

Young goats are
called kids.

The farmer takes
care of the animals
and crops.

Tractors harvest
fruits and
vegetables.

Crops grow on
a farm.

Ducklings follow
their mothers.

Sheep grow thick
hair called wool.